A POOR
GIRL
WHO
BECAME
THE
MOTHER
OF LIFE

AN INSPIRATIONAL LOOK AT THE
VIRGIN MARY, THE MOTHER OF JESUS

A POOR GIRL WHO BECAME THE MOTHER OF LIFE

KAREN T. COMFORT

Copyright © 2019 Karen Comfort

A Poor Girl Who Became the Mother of Life: An Inspirational Look at the Virgin Mary, the Mother of Jesus

All rights reserved. No portion of this book may be reproduced, stored in a retrieval system, or transmitted in any form or by any means—-electronic, mechanical, photocopy, recording, or any other—except for brief quotation in printed reviews, without prior written permission of the publisher.

Published in the U. S. A.

By ZION Publishing House, Sioux Falls, S. D. & Washington, D. C.

www.zionpublishinghouse.com

Cover illustration by Joshua M. Comfort

ISBN: 978-1-7323520-7-0 paperback
ISBN: 978-1-7323520-9-4 eBook

Scripture taken from the Holy Bible, NEW INTERNATIONAL VERSION®, NIV® Copyright © 1973, 1978, 1984, 2011 by Biblica, Inc.® Used by permission. All rights reserved worldwide.

Scripture quotations taken from the Amplified® Bible (AMPC), Copyright © 1954, 1958, 1962, 1964, 1965, 1987 by The Lockman Foundation. Used by permission. www.Lockman.org

Scripture taken from the New King James Version®. Copyright © 1982 by Thomas Nelson. Used by permission. All rights reserved.

This book is dedicated to God, my Heavenly Father. He is the Maker and Supreme Ruler of Heaven and Earth. It is also dedicated to and inspired by my earthly dad, the late Pastor Norman King. My dad truly loved the Lord! He especially loved the Word of God and had a zeal for studying and teaching the infallible truths and principles in the Word of God. He was known by all, who had the pleasure of knowing and meeting him, as a walking and living Bible. His favorite scripture, and I believe the foundational scripture for his life while on assignment here on planet earth, was II Timothy 2:15, *"Study to shew thyself approved unto God, a workman that needeth not to be ashamed, rightly dividing the word of truth"* (King James Version).

The week before my dad transitioned from his life of labor to his life of eternal reward, he shared with a few members of our family and a close friend to the family, the title of this book. He actually told us that day that he was going to be writing a book, and the title would be, "A Poor Girl Who Became the Mother of Life."

Dad, I know you are now part of that "great cloud of witnesses" referred to by the Apostle Paul in Hebrews 12:1. I thank God for you, and for the honor and the privilege to have been able to call you my dad, here in the earth realm. You were truly a "good and perfect gift" from above in every way.

TABLE OF CONTENTS

INTRODUCTION   9

Chapter 1
Your Humble Beginnings do not Determine
the Magnitude of Your Assignment   13

Chapter 2
No Matter Where You Are in Life, God Knows
Just Where to Find You   21

Chapter 3
Agree with God: You are Blessed and Highly
Favored!   25

Chapter 4
Take Courage: You Have a Great Purpose
and Assignment!   35

Chapter 5
Submit to the Will of God   57

Chapter 6
God's Will Revealed by Faith is Fulfilled!   67

Chapter 7
Song of Triumph!   79

Introduction

Too often in life, people allow their circumstances, backgrounds, education, economic class, zip code, race, sex, doubt, fear, the negative words of others, and even their own inner voice, to limit the plans Almighty God has for their lives. They wrestle with feelings and thoughts of inadequacy. They feel they are not qualified or worthy. People often lack the faith to lay hold of their God-given assignment and destiny. All these things leave too many of us, especially in the Body of Christ, feeling hopeless, unfulfilled, and living a life without purpose.

The Creator-God has given every human being in the world an earthly assignment, a purpose, and a destiny. It is recorded in the Bible, which is the Word of God. God told the prophet, Jeremiah, *"Before I formed thee in the belly I knew thee; and before thou camest forth out of the womb I sanctified thee, and I ordained thee a prophet unto the nations"* Jeremiah 1:5 (King James Version). This Word from God was not just relevant to Jeremiah. The Prophet, Jeremiah is not the only person God formed in the belly, knew, sanctified (which means to set apart), and gave a destiny to (which means a vocation). This Word from God is relevant to all His creation. It is relevant to every man, woman, boy, and girl. It is also important to understand that God's earthly assignment, purpose, and destiny for your life will always be much bigger than you will be able to accomplish on your own. This is not because He wants you to get discouraged, give up, or quit; rather, He wants you to fully rely on Him, so He gets all of the glory from your life. Revelation 4:11 says, *"Thou art worthy, O Lord, to receive glory and honour and power: for thou hast created all things, and for thy pleasure they are and were created"* (KJV). You were created for God's pleasure! And, you were created to accomplish GREAT things for the Kingdom of God here on planet Earth.

Upon close examination of the story of the Virgin Mary, the mother of Jesus the Christ (which means The Anointed One), one can see so many valuable lessons about the nature and ways of God. You can see that God is not concerned about the things men often consider when determining a person's potential. When it comes to God, your humble beginnings do not determine the magnitude of your earthly assignment. Your humble beginnings do not determine the greatness of Almighty God's call on your life. Upon examining God's calling on the Virgin Mary's life, you see that no matter where you are in life, God knows just where to find you when it's time to set His plan in motion. It's important to point out here that the phrase, "no matter where you are in life" can relate to a person's physical or spiritual location in life.

God had an extraordinary assignment for the Virgin Mary's life. He desired to use her to bring forth His plan of salvation in the person of His Only Begotten Son, Jesus the Christ. She was hand-picked by God, not man, for this life-altering and life-changing assignment. She was a poor virgin girl who became the Mother of "Life." In John 14:6, Jesus said, *"I am the way, the truth, and the life"* (KJV). Like Mary, God has an extraordinary assignment for your life!

Chapter 1

Your Humble Beginnings do not Determine the Magnitude of Your Assignment

*"And Nathanael said unto him,
Can there any good thing come out of Nazareth?
Philip saith unto him, Come and see."*

John 1:46 (KJV)

I remember like it was yesterday. My family and I, along with a close friend of the family, arrived at my parents' house from church. We had a beautiful worship service that Sunday, filled with the presence of God. We were getting ready to have church with my dad, the late Pastor Reverend Norman King, who at the time was confined to the house. After singing many hymns of praise and worship and sharing the preached Word from the Sunday service, my dad began to talk to us about the earthly mother of our Lord and Savior Jesus the Christ. He started asking us several questions.

He first asked, "What does the Bible tell us about Mary, the mother of Jesus? Specifically, what does it say about her lineage? What does it say about where she came from? And, what does it say about her class or status?" He went on to share that if you search the scriptures, it does not tell us much at all about who Mary's earthly parents were. The only relatives of Mary's the Bible mentions are her cousin Elizabeth and Elizabeth's husband Zacharias, who was a priest. Also, the scriptures tell us about Joseph to whom she was betrothed (engaged to be married to). As we pondered his questions and his insight into these truths, he further imparted to us, perhaps her lineage was not mentioned because she came from very humble, even meager or poor beginnings.

My dad was a deep thinker and always meditated on the Word of God and the things of God. During the time of his illness, he spent most of the time with his eyes closed. Looking back, I believe he was spending this time communing with God and listening to the voice of the Holy Spirit. He shared with us how amazing it was that this virgin girl of extremely humble means and beginnings would be "handpicked" by God—the Supreme Maker and Ruler of Heaven and Earth—to be the conduit through which God's redemptive plan of salvation and gift of eternal life would come to the Jews, God's chosen people, and ultimately to all man-kind! When you really stop and think about it, what was it that made the Virgin Mary so special that God would pick her to be the "Mother of Life?" It certainly was not because she was a virgin, as I am sure there were many virgin girls in the Jewish nation. It certainly was not because she was well-known, well-educated, well-liked, or even accomplished. It was not because she came from a family with great wealth or significant stature in the Jewish nation because the Bible, unlike in so many other instances, does not even mention her lineage.

However, the Gospel of Luke does trace the lineage of our Lord and Savior Jesus the Christ back through Mary, instead of Joseph, because Jesus is the Son of God. As a matter of fact, Mary and her family resided in a city of Galilee called Nazareth. It is recorded in the Bible in the Gospel of St. John 1:45-46, *Philip findeth Nathanael, and saith unto him*, *"We have found him, of whom Moses in the law, and the prophets did write, Jesus of Nazareth, the son of Joseph"* (KJV). *And Nathanaelsaid unto him*, *"Can there any good thing come out of Nazareth?"* (John 1:46, KJV). Why would Nathanael say such a thing about Nazareth and especially about Jesus before even meeting Him?

According to an excerpt by Ethan R. Longhenry from Expository Files 19.7; July 2012, Galilee itself was seen as remote, away from the epicenter of Judaism in Jerusalem, not known for education or much civilization. Within Galilee itself, Nazareth barely registers, receiving no mention from Jewish sources before the third century of our era. This insignificance led some skeptics to doubt whether Nazareth existed at all in the first century Common Era (CE), but archaeological evidence does indicate the place was inhabited. It is now believed that Nazareth was a village of no more than five-hundred people in the days when Jesus grew up there. Nazareth is about sixteen miles southwest of the Sea of Galilee; it is not near the Mediterranean Sea and would not be on a lot of travel routes. It is evident why Nazareth would easily be despised in the eyes of others; it is in the backwoods or out in the sticks, a small village. In the eyes of more educated and urban Jews, the Nazarenes would have been judged as ignorant at best and perhaps as simple-minded sinners at worst.

By all accounts and according to man's standards and rationality, Mary should never have been a consideration to bring forth the savior of God's chosen people and of all humanity—the only begotten Son of God, the King of Kings. However, seemingly from "nowhere" in Israel, God in His divine providence and infinite wisdom, predestined and chose this young teenage girl of little to no significance to mankind, to be one of the greatest women in all of history—the mother of His only begotten Son, the Mother of Life!

Another Remarkable Woman of God from Humble Beginnings

Reflecting on the Virgin Mary's story reminds me of the story of another remarkable woman of humble beginnings. Certainly, her assignment does not compare to and was not of the same magnitude as the Virgin Mary. When you think about it, there is no other woman on planet Earth whose assignment will ever compare with that of the Virgin Mary's. However, this remarkable woman's assignment was an important one, nonetheless. This remarkable woman is my mother, Lady Barbara Ellen King. My mother is the tenth of twelve children. She was born in a really small town called Aylett, in King William County, Virginia. I am sure few people have ever heard of this town. Her dad, my grandfather, worked as a foreman at a sand and gravel pit, and her mom, my grandmother, was a housewife. As a young girl, my mother grew up in the segregated South. In the year 1966, the public schools in King William County, Virginia were starting to integrate. My mother was among the few African Americans to attend King William High School, which was all-white at the time. Prior to 1966, the African-American students attended Hamilton Holmes High School. My mother was starting her senior year when she entered King William High School. My mother and another African-American, named Earl Jones, were the only two African-American seniors that year. Every day, the students at her high school called her a "black nigger" or left her a note saying, "Black nigger go back where you belong." My mother was devastated by the disrespectful, demeaning, and cruel manner in which she was treated because of her race. She would go home every day and cry.

One day, she told her dad she was not going back to that school because she could not take it anymore. She wanted to return to Hamilton Holmes High School where she had completed her freshman through junior years. Besides, that was the school where her friends were. Hamilton Holmes High School was the school from which her older siblings had graduated. However, God had another path for her. God equipped and appointed my mother for such a time in history. God also blessed my mother with supportive and God-fearing parents. My grandfather did not tolerate his daughter being treated in such a manner. He also did not raise a quitter. My grandfather went to that high school and spoke with the principal about the way my mother was being treated by the students. He also contacted the superintendent of the school board. Needless to say, the students' behavior changed. My mother ended up staying at King William High School and was the first African-American female to graduate from there. After she graduated, the public schools in King William County fully integrated.

Now, stop and really think about this story about my mother. Out of all the African- Americans in King William County, Virginia back in 1966, Almighty God "handpicked" her to be one of the first African-Americans to blaze the trail for other African-American students in King William County, Virginia to receive access to a better education.

Truly, God demonstrates through the story of the Virgin Mary and my mom, our humble beginnings do not determine the magnitude of our God-given earthly assignment, purpose, and destiny.

Chapter 2

No Matter Where You Are in Life, God Knows Just Where to Find You

"And in the sixth month the angel Gabriel was sent from God unto a city of Galilee, named Nazareth. To a virgin espoused to a man whose name was Joseph, of the house of David; and the virgin's name was Mary. And the angel came in unto her..."

St. Luke 1:26-28 (KJV)

According to biblical scholars, four hundred years had passed between the time God had delivered His final message to the nation of Israel through His prophet Malachi and the conception of the Messiah. This time period is referred to as the Intertestamental Period—the period of time between the Old Testament and the New Testament. For four hundred years God paused all communication with mankind. During this four-hundred-year span of time there were no prophets and no inspired writers of divine revelation. Also, during this time, the nation of Israel went through six eras of captivity and oppression by various nations because of their disobedience and rebellion against God. However, God was working out His plan of salvation for His chosen people and all mankind.

In the fullness of time, or at the appointed time in history, God sent Gabriel, the one who stands in God's very presence, to Nazareth to deliver a message straight from the Creator to Mary. This message was about her God-given purpose and life-changing destiny. Can you see it? Can you see Mary going about her day as usual, living in her lowly state and condition in her parent's home? She was a young, teenage girl, who was probably preparing herself to be a suitable wife to Joseph, the man to whom she was betrothed. As far as she knew, that was her only purpose in life and the only life-changing event she would experience. Then, **SUDDENLY**, in comes this glorious and magnificent being she'd never seen before! In that moment in time, her life was forever changed and would absolutely never be the same!

Interestingly, there are only two other people in all of the sixty-six books of the Bible, to whom God sent His archangel, Gabriel to deliver a message on His behalf: Daniel—one of the Old Testament major prophets (the term major prophets refers to the length and extensiveness of the books in the Bible that are inspired by specific prophets), and Zacharias, the father of John the Baptist. In both instances in the Bible when God sent His archangel, Gabriel, He revealed to these "hand-picked" individuals His divine plan that He would carry-out through and in their lives. Mary was pretty important, even in her lowly status, to the plan of God. This reminds me of what God said to the major prophet, Jeremiah in the book of Jeremiah, Chapter 1, verse 5. God told Jeremiah, *"Before I formed thee in the belly I knew thee; and before thou camest forth out of the womb I sanctified thee, and I ordained thee a prophet unto the nations"* (KJV). This was also true for Mary! Before God the Creator formed her in the belly, He also knew her, and before she came forth out of her mother's womb, God had already sanctified or "set her apart" to be the mother of our Lord and Savior, Jesus the Christ! God knew that He had ordained, appointed, and anointed this virgin, teenage girl named Mary to be the Mother of Life. Isn't that exciting?! Isn't that good news?

You might be asking, "Why is that good news?" Because, before the Creator God formed you in your mother's womb, He also knew you, and when you came forth out of your mother's womb, He also sanctified and ordained you for a great assignment, purpose, and destiny in this earth realm. It does not matter where you are in life. It does not matter what your background, such as your ethnicity, race, or nationality. It does not matter whether you are male or female. It does not matter what your social class status is according to this world's system. Your level of education does not matter. It does not matter how young or old you are. You can be in the White House, the House of Congress, the house of the rich and famous, the poor house, the jailhouse, the crack house, or no house at all! No matter where you are in life, no matter what your circumstances or your situation, no matter what your background or education, God has an extraordinary purpose and plan for your life. Believe that today! He knows just where to find you, especially when it's in the fullness of time for Him to fulfill the purpose and the assignment He has for your life.

Chapter 3

Agree With God—You Are Blessed and Highly Favored!

"And the angel came in unto her, and said, Hail, thou that art highly favoured, the Lord is with thee: blessed art thou among women."

St. Luke 1:28 (KJV)

What a salutation (greeting) by the Archangel Gabriel! What a declaration over Mary's life straight from Almighty God! Let's take a closer look at what's happening here. Gabriel comes to Mary, and the first word he says to her is, "Hail!" According to *The Strong's Exhaustive Concordance of the Bible,* the word "Hail" here is the Greek word, "Chairo," which means to "Rejoice; Be Cheerful!" Isn't that a wonderful salutation and greeting sent on God's behalf? Gabriel did not come to Mary and say, "Listen up, you lowly, peasant girl. I have a message from your Creator." Rather, Gabriel appeared to her with a warm, kind greeting from a loving, caring, and compassionate Creator to His creation. He came to bear glad tidings, to deliver a wonderful message to Mary in hopes that she would agree with the plan God had for her life. More importantly, it was not just the plan that God had for her life, but this plan was for all of mankind!

Let me take a moment here to point out this significant characteristic of God. He works on both the micro and macro-levels of our lives. His purpose and plans for our lives not only bless, impact, and transform our lives, but His purpose and plans for our lives also tremendously bless, impact, and transform the lives of others. God's plans for our lives are not all about us. Rather, He wants to use us to be a blessing to others!

Gabriel goes on to tell Mary about her real status in life, her God-given status in life, and the life to come. Gabriel tells Mary, "You are highly favoured; the Lord is with you. Blessed are you among women!" I believe it was extremely important. It was imperative for Gabriel to make this declaration to Mary. He had to enlighten her mind and heart about who she was in the sight of God, so she could embrace her God-given purpose and destiny. There are so many people who measure their significance in life, and in the sight of God based on their circumstances, situations, and status. We believe what the world's system tells us about how to assess our significance and worth in life. The world tells us we are important based on where we live, where we work, what school we attend, what degrees we earn, what we wear, and how much we make. However, God does not measure our significance and worth according to this world's system.

After Gabriel makes this declaration, it is recorded in the following passage of Scripture that Mary was troubled (greatly agitated, perplexed or disturbed) and considered (deliberated, reasoned, and disputed) in her mind about what he was saying to and about her. In other words, there was a battle, a struggle going on in her mind between what the messenger of God was declaring about her and how she viewed herself. We must remember that Mary, although "handpicked" and chosen by God to be the "Mother of Life," was also human. She was a young, teenage girl. She did not come from the upper echelon of society. She might not have even been the most beautiful or attractive of young women. I believe very strongly in my spirit that it was vitally important for Mary to understand and agree with God's declaration about her!

Look at our society today, there are so many people whom the enemy has deceived regarding who they are in the sight of God. There are men who believe they really should have been born women, and women who believe they should have been born men. Consequently, there are men walking around acting like women, and women walking around acting like men. They have been deceived! This identity confusion is a work of the adversary. The adversary tries to attack our identity, our confidence in what God says about us andabout who we truly are. The adversary wants us to have an identity crisis because if he can distort our identity, then he can destroy our God-given assignment, purpose, and destiny. The adversary even tried to tempt our Lord and Savior Jesus Christ in this very area of His life.

According to the Gospel of St. Luke, Chapter 4, after Jesus was baptized in the Jordan River, He was led by the Holy Spirit into the wilderness where he was tempted by the devil for forty days. How was the devil tempting Jesus? He was tempting Him regarding His identity. He kept saying to Jesus, "If you are the Son of God, then…" Well, Jesus fully knew that He was and is the Son of God, so He had nothing to prove to the devil, and after fully withstanding the devil's temptation, Jesus went forth in the power of the Holy Spirt into the commencement of His earthly ministry.

Before Mary could verbalize the debate and dispute going on in her mind, Gabriel told her, *"Fear not, Mary: for thou hast found favour with God."* (Luke 1:30, KJV). Why did Gabriel tell Mary, "Fear not?" I don't believe it was because Mary was afraid of Gabriel or his presence. For it is recorded in the earlier verses of Luke 1 when Gabriel appeared to the priest Zacharias, that he was perplexed, and fear fell upon him. However, in the encounter between Gabriel and Mary, it never states that fear fell upon her, only that she was troubled and considered in her mind the things that Gabriel said to her. I believe that Gabriel told Mary, "Fear not," because she had to cast down certain thoughts about herself, her status, and her circumstances that were in direct opposition to what the messenger of God was saying about her. I believe Gabriel told Mary to "Fear not" because at that moment the adversary was trying to snatch the Word that God had spoken over her from out of her heart before it could take root.

What is the opposite of fear—FAITH! Mary had to have FAITH!! She had to trust and believe what God was saying about her. Mary had to come into agreement with the TRUTH of what God had to say about her, and who she was in the sight of God. Gabriel told her three things about herself in just one sentence: 1) You are highly favored, 2) The

Lord is with you, and 3) You are blessed among all women. God has declared so many wonderful truths about us, His children, in His holy and infallible Word. All throughout the Bible, God has said things about who we are that, we too, as Mary did, have to come in agreement with, such as, Romans 8:16-17, *"The Spirit itself beareth witness with our spirit, that we are the children of God: And if children, then heirs; heirs of God, and joint-heirs with Christ..."* (KJV). Romans 8:37 says, *"... we are more than conquerors through him Christ Jesus [emphasis added] that loved us."* (KJV) And, 1 Peter 2:9, *"But ye are a chosen generation, a royal priesthood, an holy nation, a peculiar people; that ye should shew forth the praises of him who hath called you out of darkness into his marvelous light."* (KJV).

Gabriel then tells Mary she has found favor with God. The phrase "has found" is the Greek word, "heurisko" *hyoo-ris'-ko,* which means find, get, obtain, perceive, see. Mary had obtained God's favor due to her character and the condition of her heart. Her character and condition of heart were not based on who she was but rather was a result of her faith. I believe Mary had a strong relationship with God, and that she was a believer in the promise of God to deliver His people by sending the Messiah. Even in the face of what seemed to be a hopeless situation for both her and her people, the oppressive rule of both the Roman Empire and the religious sects – the Sadducees and Pharisees, she hoped in God and what He had promised through His prophets, which was her deliverance and the deliverance of her people. We too, like Mary must hold fast to our hope and confidence in God and His promises, and most importantly, we must hold fast to our relationship with God. Hebrews 10:35 admonishes us, *"Therefore do not cast away your confidence [or your hope], which has great reward."* (NKJV) We have to understand the importance of coming into agreement with God and His Word. Amos 3:3 declares, *"Can two walk together, unless they are agreed?"* (NKJV). We cannot truly say we are walking with God if we do not agree with Him. It had to be established and settled within Mary's mind and heart that which God had declared about her from the very beginning, before she arrived on planet Earth concerning who she was!

When I consider Luke 1:28 and what God said to the Virgin Mary through His messenger Gabriel, it reminds me of a time in my life when the Holy Spirit was ministering to me about a certain area of my life. God was trying to get me to move out of my own way in order to get to my next assignment. However, He had to deal with the strongholds in my mind. He had to deal with the reality that my mind was programmed according to this world's system, and the world's way of doing things. It was at a time in my life when I desired to get to the next level in my career. I was far along at this point in my career with the federal government, but I had not completed my undergraduate degree. I was going to school part-time to complete my degree and still needed to complete several credit hours. In my mind and heart, I kept saying to myself I need to complete my degree if I expect to get to the next level in my career. Besides, the people at the level to which I aspired had either an undergraduate, graduate, or doctoral degree.

BUT, there was this still small voice that kept telling me over and over again, "Karen, you can either have it your way or agree with me." The Holy Spirit kept telling me you do not need a degree to get to the next level because I have already opened the door for you to the next level. However, there was this battle still raging in my mind and heart that I needed to complete my undergraduate degree to be "qualified" or "worthy" for the next level. Then, it seemed what the Holy Spirit was ministering to me transcended all my doubts, fears, and feelings of inadequacy. I decided it was time for me to agree with God, and it was then God began to bring people into my life who made it their personal mission to help me get to the next level of my career.

God used a supervisor that I had worked for twenty years prior. Yes, I said twenty years prior. He allowed our paths to cross again, and my former supervisor became my personal mentor and champion. This divine connection with my former supervisor resulted in not only one door opening to the next level in my career but three doors opening, all at the same time. He encouraged me to interview for a position which he knew was going to open. He was certain if I applied for the position I would be among the best qualified and also get an interview. Well, he was right! I was referred as one of the best qualified and was asked to interview for the position. When I told my former supervisor that I received a request for an interview, he told me even if I did not get selected for the position, it would still be beneficial for me because the interview process would put me in front of one of the most powerful councils at the federal agency I was working for. Again, he was right! I did not get that position, and it was not because I wasn't the best qualified. Instead, I did not get that position because God had something better for me.

As my former supervisor "prophesied," as a result of the interview process, several members of the council contacted me to ask me to apply for positions in their organizations, all at the next level. I remember saying, "God, I do not know what you want me to do or which way you want me to go." He assured me any direction I went in, He was directing my path. Of course, it was exactly as God said. I ended up choosing the position that I know without a shadow of doubt was tied to my next assignment in life. And, guess what? When I entered into my new position I had not yet completed my undergraduate degree.

I want to encourage you today to agree with God and what He has to say about you. He has declared about you that which He declared about Mary and that which He has declared about me, "You are highly favored! He is with you! You are blessed!"

Chapter 4

Take Courage: You Have a Great Purpose and Assignment!

"And, behold, thou shalt conceive in thy womb, and bring forth a son, and shalt call his name JESUS. He shall be great and shall be called the Son of the Highest: and the Lord God shall give unto him the throne of his father David: And he shall reign over the house of Jacob forever; and of his kingdom there shall be no end."

St. Luke 1:31-33 KJV

I believe if we had the opportunity to interview the Virgin Mary, she would probably say like so many of us, that never in a million years would she have imagined that God would give her such a great assignment, purpose, and destiny in the earth realm. But, God had indeed! He ordained and arranged it from the very beginning of time. In the fullness of time, God revealed to the Virgin

Mary her assignment, purpose, and destiny. However, she had to be courageous enough to believe what God showed her and what God told her! Like the Virgin Mary, God has also ordained and arranged a great assignment, purpose, and destiny for our lives. We too have to be courageous enough to believe what God reveals to us and what He has to say about us.

In meditating on Mary's encounter with the Archangel Gabriel and reflecting specifically on what he said to her, five key things leap off the pages of the Bible that were important for Mary to do and to understand. As such, these five things are also vitally important for every believer to do and understand in order to grasp, lay hold of, and fulfill their God-given assignment, purpose, and destiny. The first thing the Archangel Gabriel said to Mary as it related to her assignment, purpose, and destiny was, "Behold!" Or, in other words, "See." The word *behold* here is the Greek word "idou". According to the *Vine's Complete Expository Dictionary of Old and New Testament Words,* "idou" is a verb which is in the imperative mood. The imperative mood is a verb form which makes a command or a request. *Idou* means to see, calling attention to what may be seen or heard or mentally apprehended in any way. This brings me to my first point

POINT ONE:
You cannot become or enter into what you cannot see.

I'm not talking about seeing with your natural eyes and neither was the Archangel Gabriel. I am talking about seeing with your eyes of faith. I am talking about seeing with your spiritual eyes. The purpose, assignment, and destiny that God has ordained for our lives is greater, much bigger than we could ever imagine. You will only be able to see, understand, and mentally apprehendor grasp through your "eyes of faith" what God, through the Holy Spirit, is revealing to you in this dispensation. If you try to see with your natural eyes, God's purpose, assignment, and destiny for you will never appear possible. However, according to Mark 10:27, "...***with God all things are possible***." Just look at what the Archangel Gabriel told the Virgin Mary about her purpose, assignment, and destiny. In the natural realm, it was impossible for her to conceive a child without being intimate with a man. Besides, she was not just going to conceive any child, she would conceive the Christ child! She was chosen to conceive the long-awaited Messiah, the Savior of her people and all of humanity, including her Savior! However, she would have to FIRST see in order for it to be possible for her to CONCEIVE it.

This brings me to the second, vitally important thing that Gabriel told the Virgin Mary, which is my second point. Gabriel said to the Virgin Mary that she would "conceive in [her] womb!"

POINT TWO:
Before anything can be birthed out or brought forth as an idea, an invention, or a creation, it must first be conceived.

What does it mean to conceive? According to the *Merriam-Webster Dictionary*, the word *conceive* is a verb, meaning it is an action word, and it can be defined as follows: to become pregnant with; to cause to begin; to originate; to take into one's mind; to form a conception of; and to imagine. Now, that is academia's definition of the word conceive.

While the dictionary helps us to start putting the meaning or interpretation of this word into perspective, in order to get the true revelation of its biblical meaning, we need to look at *The Strong's Exhaustive Concordance of the Bible*. The phrase "thou shalt conceive" is the Greek word "*syllambanō,*" which means to "clasp, i.e., seize, take, to take hold of (arrest, capture)." Therefore, in order to conceive, there are some actions required on our part other than just seeing. As previously mentioned, we have to first see in order to conceive. How can you clasp, seize, take or lay hold of something you cannot even see? What is the point of seeing something and then doing nothing about it? You must seize, take hold of, become pregnant with expectation, anticipation, and hope as it relates to what God shows you about who you are, and about what He's destined for your life!

One of my favorite accounts in the Bible is about Joseph. I personally identify with Joseph's life. In the Bible, Joseph was referred to as a dreamer (Genesis 37:19). He was referred to as a dreamer because God revealed his God-given purpose and assignment to him in two separate dreams. And, because Joseph was able to see it through the eyes of faith, he was able to conceive even though he went through much travail to give birth to his destiny. Many of us are familiar with Joseph's story and all he endured. As a young man, he was thrown into a pit by his own brothers; then his brothers pulled him out of the pit and sold him into slavery where he was carried down to Egypt to Potiphar's House. Potiphar's wife falsely accused him of trying to rape her which landed him in prison. But, in all of this, Joseph knew that God was with him, and he held fast to what God revealed to him about his purpose, assignment, and destiny.

I believe when the Archangel Gabriel said to the Virgin Mary, "Behold," he showed her a vision of her assignment. I believe God has shown and told you things as well. God is always speaking to His creation. He speaks to us in many ways, such as, dreams, visions, prophecies, His creation, and visitations. However, the main way He speaks to us is through His written Word—the BIBLE! I want to encourage you to spend time in the Word of God. The Word of God is like a mirror. The more we behold or see the Word of God, the more we will be able to accurately see what God has called and destined us to be and carry-out in this earth realm.

What is it you are passionate about? Is it something you really love doing and think about all of the time? Do you have a dream or aspiration in your mind and heart that seems larger than life itself? It is probably aligned to your God-given purpose and assignment. I want to encourage you to be courageous like the Virgin Mary. In reaction to this tremendous revelation about her purpose, she courageously and boldly clasped, seized, took a hold of, or in the words of the scripture, "conceived" it in her womb. She conceived it in her womb, which is the innermost part of the anatomy that brings forth life; the birthing place!

This brings me to the third, vitally important thing that Gabriel told the Virgin Mary, and my third point. Gabriel said to the Virgin Mary, "thou shalt bring forth a son!"

POINT THREE:

After you conceive, you must bring forth.

Conception is not the only necessary step in a pregnancy in order to have a baby. Conception alone is just not enough. In order to have a baby, you must nurture and take great care of the fetus as it is growing and developing inside the womb; you must carry the baby to full-term so that it is not pre-mature; and then you must bring forth or "birth out" the baby. When you are having a baby, you do not go right from conception to birthing. In other words, there is a necessary process in between conception and birthing. It is the gestation process.

In the natural, when a woman is pregnant, she goes through what are referred to as trimesters. Interestingly, there are three trimesters in a pregnancy, each of which is marked by specific fetal developments. Each trimester is divided into twelve weeks, or three months for a total of forty weeks, until it is time for the baby to be born. Both the numbers 3 and 40 have biblical significance. The number three represents completeness. It also represents the Holy Trinity – God the Father, God the Son, and God the Holy Spirit. Man, like the Holy Trinity, is a Triune being. Man is a spirit, he has a soul, and he lives in a body. The number forty represents a period of testing, trial, and judgment in order to fulfill God's promises. It's interesting that the natural process through which a fetus develops, grows, and then is ready to be born has spiritual significance and can be pointed to as the same spiritual birthing process for our divine purpose, assignment, and destiny.

According to the University of California San Francisco's Medical Center, the first trimester is the most crucial to the baby's development. During this period, the baby's body structure and organ systems develop. Most miscarriages and birth defects occur during the first trimester. It is usually the most difficult trimester for the expecting mother because it's when she experiences what is referred to as "morning sickness." The same is also true for the spiritual baby, which is your God-given purpose, assignment, and destiny. When it begins to grow and develop in you, it is vitally important during the "first trimester" to continue to hold fast and to seize and clasp that which God through the Holy Spirit has shown and told you. It is vitally important to do this, so you do not miscarry or unintentionally "abort" your spiritual baby. You have to nurture and protect your spiritual baby.

How do you do this? Well, how does a pregnant woman naturally nurture and protect her unborn fetus? She nourishes herself and the unborn fetus with healthy foods. She takes prenatal vitamins and sees her obstetrics and gynecology (OB-GYN) doctor on a regular basis. She spends time around other pregnant women. She gets adequate rest, and she stops or does not start doing things that would harm her unborn fetus. Similarly, you must nourish yourself and your spiritual baby with the Word of God daily. The Word of God is you and your spiritual baby's food and vitamins. According to Luke 4:4, Jesus said, *"It is written, that man shall not live by bread alone, but by every word of God."* (New King James Version). You must also spend time in prayer, praise, and worship. You need to get around Bible-believing and like-minded women and men of

God. You must abide, remaining stable and fixed, under the shadow of the Almighty God in the secret place (Psalm 91:1). This is a place of complete submission to God's authority and His protective presence. God, in the person of His Holy Spirit, will be your Obstetrician and Gynecologist (OB-GYN), and will lead, guide, and instruct you during this very critical time.

There are two excellent examples in the Scriptures of what we, as believers, should do once we have "conceived" our God-given purpose and assignment and our spiritual babies are going through the "gestation" process. The first example is of the Virgin Mary herself. Once the Archangel Gabriel told Mary about her God-given purpose and assignment, it is recorded in Luke 1:39-40, *"Now Mary arose in those days and went into the hill country with haste, to a city of Judah, and entered the house of Zacharias and greeted Elizabeth."* (NKJV). Mary did not rise up and quickly go tell her parents, her neighbors, her best friends, or even the man to whom she was betrothed about her God-given purpose and assignment. She went to her cousin Elizabeth, whom at that time was six months pregnant with John the Baptist, the forerunner of Jesus Christ—whom Mary was now impregnated with. Further, the Bible says in the 41st verse of Luke Chapter 1, when Elizabeth heard the salutation of Mary, the babe in Elizabeth's womb leaped, and Elizabeth was filled with the Holy Spirit. Not only that, Elizabeth confirmed what the Archangel Gabriel had just told Mary saying, *"Blessed art thou among women, and blessed is the fruit of thy womb."* (KJV). Mary knew that she could not tell just anyone about her pregnancy.

First of all, she was pregnant out of wed-lock. Although she was betrothed (engaged) to Joseph, which according to Jewish custom was the same as being married, she had not consummated the marriage covenant with Joseph. In other words, she had had no sexual relations with Joseph. Therefore, it could have been assumed that she had been unfaithful to Joseph with another man. And, in accordance with Jewish law and custom, Mary could have been stoned to death. She and her baby could have been killed. However, Mary was led by the Holy Spirit to go to her cousin Elizabeth's house. Her cousin Elizabeth's house represented a safe-haven for Mary and her baby. Mary's cousin Elizabeth represented like-minded individuals who see, conceive, and walk in their God-given purpose. Her cousin Elizabeth represented people of God who also see your God-given purpose, assignment, and destiny, and these people encourage you; they speak words of faith to you; they pray with you;

they stand with you; and they praise and worship with you to nurture and protect your spiritual baby. These individuals don't just see your God-given purpose, assignment, and destiny as a blessing to you, but they see how it's a blessing and a necessity to the fulfillment of the Kingdom of God and the Body of Christ. They see how your God-given purpose and assignment is a blessing to them!

According to Luke 1:56, Mary stayed with her cousin Elizabeth for about three months, then returned to her own house. Mary stayed with her cousin until her first trimester was completed. As previously mentioned, the first trimester is the most crucial trimester in the development of the baby's body structure and organ systems, and most miscarriages and birth defects occur during this period.

The second example is that of our Lord and Savior Jesus the Christ. In Luke 3:21-22 (KJV), it is recorded, *"Now when all the people were baptized, it came to pass, that Jesus also being baptized, and praying, the heaven was opened. And the Holy Ghost descended in a bodily shape like a dove upon him, and a voice came from heaven, which said, Thou art my beloved Son; in thee I am well pleased."*

For Jesus, this was the time of conception of His earthly ministry. The heavenly Father told His only begotten son that thou [Jesus] are my beloved Son. After Jesus "conceives," He is led, according to the 4th Chapter of the Gospel of Luke, by the Spirit into the wilderness where he is tempted for forty days by the devil. Notice the number 40 again. As previously mentioned, the number forty represents a period of testing, trial, and judgment in order to fulfill God's promises. Even Jesus had to go through the "gestation" process before His earthly ministry went forth or was "birthed." Jesus had to be prepared and "powered-up." In the wilderness, the devil tested, tempted, and tried to attack Jesus' identity. Jesus' identity was tied to His earthly purpose, assignment, and ultimate destiny.

The heavenly Father told Jesus that He was His beloved Son. Jesus is the only begotten Son of God who was sent to redeem mankind back to the Father. Jesus was the sacrificial Lamb of God who was sent to take away the sins of the world. He was sent to ransom us from the wages of sin, which according to Romans 6:23, is "death." And, it is recorded in Luke 4:3, that the first thing the devil said to Jesus was, "If thou be the Son of God." The enemy will test, tempt, and try to attack the Word and the declaration that God has spoken to us regarding our purpose, assignment, and destiny. The enemy tested, tempted, and tried to attack Jesus three times, and each time, Jesus responded with the Word of God! If Jesus fought the enemy with the Word of God, then it is imperative for us to also use the Word of God to fight the enemy. The enemy is after your God-given purpose, assignment, and destiny. And, Jesus is our greatest role model. He came and walked this earth to show us how to be victorious in this life.

I chose these two examples because Mary took a certain course of action, as outlined above, in the beginning of her "gestation" period to nurture and protect herself and her baby—Jesus. And, Jesus took a certain course of action as He was going through His "gestation" period and was ready to "birth" out the commencement of His earthly ministry. Jesus' forty days was a time of travailing. He was going through "birth pangs". Jesus had to bear down and stand His ground against the enemy who came to test, tempt, and attack Him when He was tired and hungry.

This portrayal of Jesus is symbolic of a woman who is ready to give birth to her newborn baby. She typically endures labor pains for hours—one contraction after the other. In some instances, when a woman is having a baby for the first time, she is in labor for many days. She is tired and worn down due to the intensity and length of each contraction. She's hungry because, for hours, or even days, she has not been allowed to have anything to eat or drink. She is so ready to push and finally get the baby out, but she is not able to "birth" the baby until her cervix has dilated ten centimeters. Sometimes the labor pains are so unbearable that some women give up. The first trimester and the last trimester are the most uncomfortable times during the gestation period.

The enemy wants you to give up! But, I want to encourage you to look to the Virgin Mary as an example. More importantly, I encourage you to look unto Jesus the Christ, Who is according to Hebrews 12:2, *"the author and the finisher of our faith."* After the devil had ended all his temptations and gave Jesus his best shot, he departed from Jesus for a season. After which, Jesus returned in the power of the Spirit into Galilee, and the news about Him spread through all the region round about (Luke 4:13-14 KJV).

This brings me to the fourth, vitally important thing the Archangel Gabriel told the Virgin Mary, and my fourth point. Gabriel said to Mary in Luke 1:31 (KJV), *"...and shalt call his name JESUS."*

POINT FOUR:
Your destiny shall have a specific name!

Do you know that there is power and significance in a name? In the Bible, every individual's name has a meaning and reveals something about their character, as well as their purpose, assignment, and destiny. When the Archangel Gabriel came to tell Mary that she would conceive in her womb and bring forth a son, he did not stop there. Honestly, when you really think about it, he could not have stopped there. If he had stopped there, then his assignment would have been incomplete. If he had stopped there, Mary would not have understood the magnitude of her purpose, assignment, and destiny. She certainly would not have understood why conceiving in her womb and bringing forth a son made her highly favored and blessed among women. Gabriel had to reveal the name of the son she would bring forth. It was the name of the son she would conceive in her womb and bring forth that would reveal the magnitude of her purpose, assignment, and destiny!

Therefore, the Archangel Gabriel had to tell Mary her son's name. The Archangel Gabriel told

Mary that she shall call her son's name JESUS. According to *The Strong's Exhaustive Concordance of the Bible*, the name Jesus means "Jehovah is Salvation." Mary was the mother of "Jehovah is Salvation!" Mary's purpose, assignment, and destiny was to conceive, carry for forty weeks, and bring forth *Jehovah is Salvation*! Selah! Just ponder on that for a moment.

When you are in Christ, it is imperative for you to recognize and know that your God-given purpose, assignment, and destiny has a specific name. Ephesians 2:10 (KJV) tells us, *"For we are his workmanship, created in Christ Jesus unto good works,* **which God hath before ordained that we should walk in them."** The "good works which God hath before ordained that we should walk in them" are our assignments, purposes, and destinies. My assignment, purpose, and destiny is not the same as your assignment, purpose, and destiny. The Virgin Mary's assignment, purpose, and destiny was not the same as our assignments, purposes, and destinies. Each of us has a purpose, assignment, and destiny with a specific name which has been designed just for us. Hallelujah! That is why we do not have to be jealous of anyone else's purpose, assignment, and destiny. We just need to recognize and understand our own assignment, purpose, and destiny, and then walk in it!

This brings me to the final vitally important thing the Archangel Gabriel told the Virgin Mary, and my fifth point. Gabriel said to Mary in Luke 1:32 (KJV), *"He shall be great..."*

POINT FIVE:
Your destiny shall be great!

The Archangel Gabriel told Mary that her son Jesus shall be great! Because she was handpicked by God to be the mother of Jesus, *she* would also be great! It is important to know when God reveals His destiny for your life, He is going to be clear about what you will call it and also the magnitude of it. Another important thing to understand about your God-given destiny is it will always be much bigger than you! Your assignment, purpose, and destiny will always be greater than either you or I have the capacity, capability, knowledge, wisdom, resources, and skills to make happen on our own. God designed it that way, so we will always fully rely on Him, and also so that He gets all of the honor, glory, and praise, which all belongs to Him anyway.

Back in September 2006, when a fire started in our family home, it was an extremely devastating time for us. I remember it like it happened yesterday. My children's faces were covered with despair, anxiety, and so much devastation. At the time, my youngest son, Joshua was eight years old. At this very young age, he would pray the most powerful and profound prayers. I recall when he prayed at church, our church family was amazed that such a young person prayed such fervent prayers. In every one of his prayers, Joshua would always ask God to take care of the homeless.

My family and I stayed with my parents while our house was being repaired from the damage caused by the fire and by the water from the sprinkler system. One day, after returning from school, Joshua handed me a picture of a beautiful house he had drawn. Across the top of his picture he wrote these words, "Homes for the Homeless." When Joshua handed me the picture, I began to talk to God about it. I said, "God, Joshua has such a burden for the homeless on him for being such a little person." I also imagined he, too was feeling a sense of homelessness. I imagined in the back of his mind he must have wondered if he would ever return to the place he had resided since the day he was born. He must have wondered if he would ever return to the place he affectionately called "home."

The Holy Spirit responded to me and told me that the picture was a vision according to Habakkuk 2:2 (KJV), which says *"And the LORD answered me, and said, write the vision, and make it plain upon tables, that he may run that readeth it."* The Holy Spirit revealed to me that my little boy Joshua had written the vision and that I was the one reading it. Therefore, I was tasked with running with the vision. The Holy Spirit revealed to me that the vision was of a non-profit organization that my family and I were assigned to establish that would help families who lost their homes due to fire, water, or natural disaster by providing them temporary housing, counseling, and other services. In addition, the Holy Spirit revealed to me that the **name** of the non-profit organization would be called, "Joshua House Ministries, Inc."

The name of the non-profit organization was important! Although, at the time the Holy Spirit revealed all of this to me, the non-profit organization did not exist in the natural realm. However, it already existed in the supernatural realm. For me, knowing the name of the non-profit organization allowed me to focus and gave me clarity concerning this assignment. The name made the non-profit organization tangible. I could clearly see and articulate the vision because I knew what to call it!

The Bible refers to this as faith. According to Hebrews 11:1 (KJV), *"Faith is the substance of things hoped for; the evidence of things not seen."* The Word of God tells us in Genesis 1:26 that we were made in the image and in the likeness of God, who according to Romans 4:17 (KJV), *"...calleth those things which be not as though they were."* Not long after Joshua handed me his drawing with the vision of the "homes for the homeless," and after the Holy Spirit revealed to me that it was a non-profit and gave me the name for it, I founded, "Joshua House Ministries, Inc."

What has God told you about your purpose, assignment, and destiny? Has God, through the person of the Holy Spirit, revealed to you what you should call it? If not, you need to press into Him and ask Him to reveal it to you. It's not just enough to know you have a purpose, assignment, and destiny. God not only wants to reveal to you what it is but also what you shall call it. What you call it will reveal the magnitude, the greatness, and the Kingdom impact your assignment, purpose, and destiny will have in this earth realm! When you know the name of your destiny, it becomes real and tangible to you. And, believe me when I say, YOUR DESTINY SHALL BE GREAT!

Chapter 5

Submit to the Will of God

"And Mary said, "Behold the handmaid of the Lord: be it unto me according to thy word."
St. Luke 1:38 (KJV)

There are so many beautiful lessons in the story about the Virgin Mary's revelation about her God-given purpose, assignment, and destiny and the prophecy concerning the birth of Jesus the Christ. Mary's story is about a woman of great faith, courage, and humility. In the face of uncertainty, even potential danger and adversity, Mary humbled herself and submitted to the will of the Almighty God, her Creator. As we see in Luke 1:38 (KJV), Mary says "*Behold the handmaid of the Lord; be it unto me according to thy word.*" Mary could have had a very different response because we all have the freedom to make our own choices. The freedom to make our own choices is known as *free-will* which God has given to every one of us.

Mary could have given the Archangel Gabriel a bunch of excuses as to why she could not be the mother of the Messiah of God's chosen people. She could have been selfish instead of selfless. She could have asked for additional time to think about if she really wanted to be a partner with God in His plan of salvation. Her life was most certainly about to be changed drastically, forever.

Instead, Mary quickly realized and clearly understood what we all must realize and understand—that is, we are all God's created works. Ephesians 2:10 (AMPC) says, *"For we are God's [own] handiwork (His workmanship), recreated in Christ Jesus, [born anew] that we may do those good works which God predestined (planned beforehand) for us [taking paths which He prepared ahead of time], that we should walk in them [living the good life which He prearranged and made ready for us to live]."* Mary said to Gabriel, *"Behold the handmaid of the Lord."*

According to *The New Strong's Exhaustive Concordance of the Bible,* the Greek word for handmaid is *doulē,* which means a female slave, bondmaid, one who worships God and submits to Him. It means one who gives himself or herself up wholly to another's will or dominion. If you look up the word *submit* in the dictionary, this is the exact definition of the word. Mary submitted herself completely to the will and the plan of God—spirit, soul, and body. She not only told the messenger of God she was the handmaid of the Lord, but she followed by saying, "be it unto me according to thy word." Even though Mary rationally or physically could not comprehend or fathom how the prophetic word concerning her life and future would ultimately play out or come to pass, she did not concern herself with those things. She fully surrendered her will to the will of Almighty God! My friends, leaving the details of our lives totally up to the will and plan of God, takes **GREAT** faith, courage, and humility.

All God wanted Mary to do was submit to Him—to His will, to His plan, and His Kingdom work. That is all God wants for you and me. It amazes me that God who is our Creator, sustainer, and keeper chooses to use us, chooses to partner with us in order to carry out His carefully orchestrated plans. There are so many times when God reveals His plans concerning our lives to us, and we get so wrapped up in needing to know the details and how He could possibly bring His plans to pass. Instead, we just need to submit, surrender, and give ourselves up wholly to the will, lordship, and dominion of God.

Let's take a closer examination of Mary, her situation, and the following three beautiful lessons from her story.

LESSON ONE:
Your life is not your own

The first important lesson for us to recognize is that at a young age, this teenage girl from Nazareth **understood that her life was not her own**. At a young age, she understood that God had need of her. Mary was not like the prophet Jeremiah, who gave God an excuse about being a child when God called him. In Jeremiah 1:6, Jeremiah told God, *"...Ah, Lord God! Behold, I cannot speak: for I am a child"* (KJV). This was Jeremiah's response when God told him that He ordained Jeremiah as a prophet unto the nations.

Mary was not caught up in what she planned to be when she grew up or what she needed to accomplish before she gave her life completely to God. She was not caught up on letting the good times roll first and then giving her life completely to God. Too many times, too many people want to give God the leftovers of their lives. They make excuses that they are not ready or need to get themselves together before they can serve God or live for Him. Then after they get older, they make excuses that they are too old to be involved in this or that ministry. Or, they make the excuse that the work of the ministry requires too much energy, time, and effort. Mary could have easily said to the Archangel Gabriel, "Well I was thinking I'd like to give birth to the Messiah after I am married and have my own children with Joseph." And, if she had, then she would have missed out on the greatest assignment and blessing of her life.

She would have no longer been **qualified** to bring forth the Messiah because she would have no longer been a virgin. God not only wanted to use Mary for His glory, but He wanted her first-fruit. He wanted the best of her life. He wanted the first-fruit of her womb. The first born in the Jewish custom was the one who was considered blessed. They were the ones who had the birthright and the spiritual and physical inheritance. Isn't that just like God? I am specifically referring to God's nature and character. Mary understood this, which is the second beautiful lesson of her story.

LESSON TWO:
God wants your very best!

When God asks us for something or to do something for Him—He asks for, wants, and expects our very best. It must mean something to us in order for it to mean something to God!

Mary came from very meager and humble beginnings. Consequently, she did not have anything of materialistic value to give up. She did not have wealth or fortune. However, she did have her life and a planned future with Joseph, her fiancé, ahead of her. She gave herself and her future to God, which was all she had and the best she had to offer. It's not hard to submit, to yield, or to give ourselves up wholly to something or someone when it's not a true sacrifice and doesn't cost us anything.

I am reminded of the story in the Bible about the rich young ruler, which can be found in all three synoptic gospels—Matthew, Mark, and Luke. I will refer to the account in Mark 10:17-22 (NKJV), which records that as Jesus was going out on the road, the rich young ruler came running and knelt before Him. Sounds really good so far—doesn't it? This rich young ruler comes running after Jesus and kneels—shows reverence and humbles himself. He then asks Jesus the following question, *"Good Teacher, what shall I do that I may inherit eternal life?"* Sounding even better—right? However, the conversation that ensues between Jesus and the rich young ruler reveals the heart of the matter. *"So, Jesus said to him, "Why do you call Me good? No one is good but One, that is, God. You know the commandments: 'Do not commit adultery,' 'Do not murder,' 'Do not steal,' 'Do not bear false witness,' 'Do not defraud,' 'Honor your father and your mother.' " And he answered and said to Him, "Teacher, all these things I have kept from my youth." Then Jesus, looking at him, loved him, and said to him, "One thing you lack: Go your way, sell whatever you have and give to the poor, and you will have treasure in heaven; and come, take up the cross, and follow Me." But he was sad at this word, and went away sorrowful, for he had great possessions.* The rich young ruler thought that keeping the commandments since he was a youth was giving God his best. However, it was not his very best! Jesus told him even with keeping the commandments all his life he was still lacking. He still was coming up short in the God's eyes. He was still holding back the very best he had to give God.

The rich young ruler loved his great possessions more than giving it all up to follow God's plans for his life.

Like Mary, we need to quickly come to the realization and revelation that this life is not all about us; rather it's all about God! This life is about giving God our very best. When we come into this realization and revelation, then we, too will be able to submit without hesitation to God's perfect will for our lives.

The next beautiful lesson we need to see about Mary's story is that she understood as we, too must understand that God's Word is His will.

LESSON THREE:
God's Word is God's will.

If we want to know the will of God, then we must know the Word of God. We must be able to discern and recognize the voice of God. God tells us His will through both His *rhēma* or spoken Word, and His *logos* or written Word. Mary told Gabriel after he told her that she would carry the Son of God, "...*be it done unto me according to thy* *word*" (Luke 1:38, KJV). Or in other words, "*Be it done unto me according to thy will.*" Let me clarify that it was not Gabriel's word or will. It was according to God's Word because Gabriel was sent to deliver God's message. Gabriel was God's messenger. However, Mary knew this and was saying to God, as our Lord and Savior would say to His Heavenly Father in the Garden of Gethsemane, "*not my will, but thy will be done.*" Isn't that amazing?! Mary, the Mother of Jesus, would in essence utter the same words to the Creator God concerning the birth of Jesus into this world as Jesus, her son, would utter to God, His Heavenly Father, concerning His death on the cross and exit out of this world. Both Mary and Jesus fully surrendered to the will of God for their lives. Hallelujah! I am so glad they did because God used them both as His holy vessels through which He wrought His plan for our salvation.

Chapter 6

God's Will Revealed, By Faith is Fulfilled!

*"Blessed is she who believed,
for there will be a fulfillment of those things
which were told her from the Lord."*

St. Luke 1:45 (KJV)

The Gospel of Luke records that after the Archangel Gabriel told everything to Mary that God had sent him to tell her, Mary said to Gabriel, *"Behold the handmaid of the Lord; be it unto me according to thy word"* (Luke 1:38, KJV). After which, the angel departed from her. Then, Mary arose and went into the hill country with haste, to a city of Judah! Mary had just experienced and been in the very presence of God by way of the visitation of Gabriel, the messenger sent from the throne room of God. Not only had she experienced and been in the very presence of God, but she had also received a word from God regarding His purpose, assignment, and destiny for her life. And, she submitted herself completely to the will of God by saying "be it unto me according to thy Word." Therefore, knowing God's will had been revealed, and that she had come into agreement by faith believing that it was fulfilled, Mary went in a hurry to a place called Praise!

The word Judah is of Hebrew origin and means "Praise" or "He shall be praised!" Mary did not have to wait until she saw the end of God's revelation to give Him praise. She did not have to wait until she saw what the Archangel Gabriel told her to manifest in order for her to believe God. She knew that it was already done! She believed it was already settled. Why? Because God revealed what He planned to do; and she came in agreement with God by faith. She laid hold of the will of God for her life by faith. Hebrews 11:1 says, *"Now faith is the substance of things hoped for, the evidence of things not seen"* (KJV). Hebrews 11: 6 says, *"But without faith it is impossible to please [or come into agreement-emphasis added] him: for he that cometh to God must believe that He is and that He is a rewarder of them that diligently seek Him"* (KJV). What is faith? Faith is confidence, trust, and reliance on God and God's Word. Faith is what was demonstrated by God when He spoke the world into existence. God believed that every time He said, "Let there be…" that it was going to come to pass, and it did.

This brings me to the first point of this chapter:

POINT ONE:
When you believe God's Word, praise Him like it's already done!

When God reveals His will for our lives, like Mary, we need to immediately come in agreement with Him by our faith in Him, and then seal it with our PRAISE! Let's look at what happens when Mary, this great woman of faith, this great woman of courage, this chosen vessel of God, arrives to this city of Judah! When she arrives to this place of "He shall be praised," it is recorded in Luke 1:39-44 that Mary entered the house of Zacharias and greeted her cousin Elizabeth. If you read Luke 1:5-25, you will see that according to the Word of God, Zacharias and his wife Elizabeth were both righteous (or in right standing) before God, walking blamelessly in all the commandments and requirements of the Lord. But, they had no children because Elizabeth was barren, and they both were advanced in age and past childbearing years. However, God sent Gabriel to reveal His will for Zacharias' and Elizabeth's lives.

God sent Gabriel to tell Zacharias that his petition had been answered and that his wife Elizabeth was going to bear him a son, whose name must be called John. In Chapter 4 of this book, my fourth point was, "Your destiny shall have a specific name." It was important for Zacharias and Elizabeth to know their son's name because their son's destiny was part of God's assignment for Zacharias' and Elizabeth's lives. According to *The New Strong's Exhaustive Concordance of the Bible,* the name John means, "Jehovah is a gracious giver." John, also known as John the Baptist, was born to be the forerunner for Jesus the Christ—the one who would prepare the way for the coming of the Savior of the world. Zachariah and Elizabeth were handpicked to bring forth Jesus Christ's forerunner!

When Mary went to see her cousin Elizabeth, Elizabeth was already six months pregnant and living in the city of Judah. Elizabeth was already at the place of "He shall be praised!" The Bible says when Elizabeth heard Mary's greeting, the babe in Elizabeth's womb leaped, and Elizabeth was filled with the Holy Spirit. Then, Elizabeth began to prophecy to Mary speaking the same words that God's messenger the Archangel Gabriel spoke unto Mary. Luke 1:42 says that Elizabeth spoke in a loud voice saying to Mary, *"Blessed are you among women, and blessed is the fruit of your womb!"* (NKJV).

My brothers and sisters in Christ, God will always confirm His spoken Word concerning our lives. According to II Corinthians 13:1, it is written *"...In the mouth of two or three witnesses shall every word be established"* (KJV). Mary went to Elizabeth's house because both women had a reason to PRAISE God, and God wanted to confirm the Word He revealed to Mary through Gabriel. Why? God's revealed will for Elizabeth's life was connected to God's revealed will for Mary's life. These two women not only had a familial connection, they also had a divine connection. If you only look at this account from a physical aspect or on the surface, it would make sense for Mary to go to Elizabeth's house after receiving the revelation from God concerning His will for her life. After all, Elizabeth was Mary's older cousin.

According to historical accounts, Elizabeth's and Mary's mothers were sisters. Also, Elizabeth was much older than Mary. Their relationship has often been compared to that of a younger and older sister. However, it was their divine connection that led Mary to visit her cousin Elizabeth. As previously mentioned, the baby in Elizabeth's womb was John the Baptist, the forerunner for Jesus the Christ. The baby's assignment in Elizabeth's womb was connected to the baby's assignment in Mary's womb. That's deep! God revealed His will to these two women who He handpicked to work out His greatest plan! The plan of the salvation of mankind.

This brings me to my second point:

POINT TWO:
God's assignment for your life has divine connections.

What we must understand about God is that His will and assignment for our lives are always much bigger than us. When God chooses to use us, we must remember that it is not about us, rather it is truly all about Him! There are so many people who are connected to us, who will be impacted by us, and who will benefit from God's plan for our lives. In the case of both Mary and Elizabeth, the assignments on their lives involved the salvation of God's chosen people, the nation of Israel, and the salvation of all mankind. The magnitude of God's assignment on our lives is why it is vitally important to have faith (confidence, trust, and reliance) in what God reveals concerning His will for our lives! Faith moves His will from *revealed* to *fulfilled*. It does not matter what the circumstances of our lives might look like. What is vitally important is for us to have faith in God!

Previously, I mentioned that according to Luke 1:5-25, God sent His Archangel Gabriel to tell Zacharias that his wife Elizabeth would bear him a son, whose name must be called John. It is recorded in these passages of scripture that when Zacharias saw Gabriel, he was troubled, and FEAR took possession of him. Not only that, when Gabriel revealed God's will concerning the birth of John the Baptist, Zacharias responded with unbelief. Since it was vitally important that God's plan of salvation be carried out in accordance with His will, the angel of God had to silence Zacharias! God cannot work with fear, doubt, and unbelief. It was that same spirit of doubt and unbelief that had put Zacharias' forefathers in a position of disobedience and rebellion against Almighty God, As I mentioned in Chapter 2, four hundred years had passed between the time God had delivered His final message to the nation of Israel through His prophet

Malachi, and the conception of the Messiah. This period of time is referred to as the Intertestamental Period—the period of time between the Old Testament and the New Testament. For four hundred years, God paused all communication with mankind. During this four-hundred-year span of time there were no prophets, no inspired writers of divine revelation, and no angelic messengers. Also, during this time, the nation of Israel went through six eras of captivity and oppression by various nations because of their disobedience and rebellion against God. At the time of Gabriel's visitation to Zacharias, the nation of Israel was under the rule of the Roman emperor. The nation of Israel's disobedience and rebellion was a result of their doubt and unbelief in God's Word, and it was that spirit that had to be silenced!

However, in direct contrast to Zacharias, when the Archangel Gabriel appeared to the Virgin Mary, the Bible does not record that fear took possession of Mary. Rather, Mary was perplexed by the Archangel Gabriel's salutation concerning her and wondered what it meant. After the Archangel Gabriel revealed God's plan to Mary, she responded with a question, which was one of wonder and curiosity but not of doubt and unbelief. When the Archangel Gabriel revealed how God's will would be carried out, Mary responded with faith and submission to God's will. Then, the Archangel Gabriel not only revealed God's will for Mary's life, he also told Mary that her cousin Elizabeth was six months pregnant. The Archangel Gabriel revealed that there was a divine connection between Elizabeth (she who had been barren) and Mary (she who was a virgin). In both women's situations, what the Archangel Gabriel revealed in the natural appeared to be impossible. However, Almighty God was performing the miraculous in and through both women's lives. According to Luke 1:37, one of my favorite scriptures in the Bible, *"For with God nothing shall be impossible"* (KJV).

There are so many divine connections of both men and women recorded all throughout the Word of God; such as, Moses and Joshua, Naomi and Ruth, and Elijah and Elisha. The divine connection I want to focus on here is the one between Moses and Joshua. According to Exodus 3:5-10 (KJV), God revealed to Moses that He had seen the affliction of His people who were in bondage in Egypt, and God heard their cry because of the harsh and severe labor Pharaoh and the Egyptians subjected them to. God revealed to Moses that He had come down to deliver the Israelites out of the hand of the Egyptians, and bring them up out of that land unto the land of Canaan, which was the land God had promised to his forefathers—to Abraham, Isaac, and Jacob. Moreover, God revealed that He chose Moses to perform this assignment in the Earth. But, because Moses disobeyed one of God's commands, Moses was stripped of the opportunity to lead God's people into the Promised Land. Instead, Joshua led them in!

Who was Joshua? According to Joshua 1:1, Joshua was the son of Nun and Moses' minister or personal servant. There are several accounts in the Bible of Joshua's divine connection to Moses. Specifically, the Bible makes known in Exodus 33:11, that as a young man, Joshua remained in the Tent of the Lord (which also means the Temple of the Lord). In Exodus 24:13 and 32:17, it is recorded that Joshua was with Moses on Mount Sinai when God gave Moses the tablets of stone with the Ten Commandments. Numbers 14 gives the account that Joshua was one of the twelve spies that Moses sent to explore and scout out the land of Canaan. Both these men of God had divine destinies that were divinely connected. As Joshua's instructor and trainer, Moses was used by God to lead His people out of the land of bondage—out of Egypt. However, it would be Joshua, Moses' minister, who God would use to lead His people into the land of promise, Canaan. God's assignment for Moses' and Joshua's lives were connected to His divine destiny for an entire people, the nation of Israel.

What a beautiful correlation of the divine connection between Elizabeth and Mary, and the divine connection between Moses and Joshua! Elizabeth gave birth to John the Baptist, who was the forerunner for Jesus Christ. John the Baptist was used to get the nation of Israel to realize they were in bondage to sin and needed a savior. He was used as a voice *crying in the wilderness* that they needed to repent (change their way of thinking) about how they were living their sinful lives. He was used to provoke them to change their desires, be free from their bondage, and turn to the Promised One. The Promised One was Jesus, the Messiah! John the Baptist could not deliver the nation of Israel out of bondage. However, he led them to the Promised One. He prepared their hearts, minds, will, and emotions to receive their King, their Deliverer, and their Savior! Just like John the Baptist, Moses was used by God to lead His people out of a place or condition of bondage. However, it was Joshua that God used to lead His people into the Promised Land. It's interesting that both Jesus' and Joshua's names have the same meaning, "Jehovah Saves!" Moses and Joshua were a type or foreshadow of John the Baptist and Jesus the Christ!

I pray that you will take courage in the divine connections presented in this chapter, and like Elizabeth, Mary, Moses, and Joshua, step out on faith. Believe God's will for your life so that it will indeed be fulfilled!

Chapter 7

Song of Triumph!

"The Song of Mary"

And Mary said:
"My soul magnifies the Lord,
And my spirit has rejoiced in God my Savior.
For He has regarded the lowly state of His maidservant;
For behold, henceforth all generations will call me blessed.
For He who is mighty has done great things for me,
And holy is His name.
And His mercy is on those who fear Him
From generation to generation.
He has shown strength with His arm;
He has scattered the proud in the imagination of their hearts.
He has put down the mighty from their thrones,
And exalted the lowly.
He has filled the hungry with good things,
And the rich He has sent away empty.
He has helped His servant Israel,
In remembrance of His mercy,
As He spoke to our fathers,
To Abraham and to his seed forever."
Luke 1:46-55 (NKJV)

Have you ever experienced such a magnificent blessing, victory, or revelation from God that it caused you to sing? I, personally have experienced this! There are also so many other people in the Bible who experienced this. For example, King David, who wrote just about half of the book of Psalms, many of his Psalms were songs. They were songs about how God had given him the victory over his enemies. Another example is a woman named Hannah. Hannah was barren and earnestly desired a son from God. According to I Samuel 1:10-11 (NKJV), Hannah was greatly distressed, and she prayed to the LORD and wept in anguish. She made a vow, saying, *"O LORD of hosts, if You will indeed look on the affliction of Your maidservant and remember me, and not forget Your maidservant, but will give Your maidservant a male child, then I will give him to the LORD all the days of his life, and no razor shall come upon his head."* God answered Hannah's prayer! In I Samuel 2, we find Hannah's song of thanksgiving and victory to God over her barren situation.

As I mentioned, I, too experienced this the year my home caught on fire. During that time, it seemed like my family and I were going through a great attack by the adversary. In addition to our home catching on fire, my physical health was under attack. At the beginning of 2006, I went to the emergency room because I was feeling awful. I had what seemed to be a really bad cold that just would not go away. The doctors kept putting me on antibiotics, but nothing seemed to work. After a series of tests, the emergency room doctors came back with an unsettling report, and I was referred to a specialist who recommended surgery. This was a very dark time in my life. My children were very young, and I did not want them to grow up without me. I really pressed into God during this time, seeking His face through prayer and meditating on His Word about what I should do. I never had peace about moving forward with the surgery, and so I never had it. The more time I spent in prayer and in the Word of God, the better I began to feel with each passing day. My health began to improve. I know that the restoration of my health was an absolute miracle from God.

It was during this time of seeking God's face and visibly seeing my health improve,, I began to write several songs to God, such as, "To You Be the Glory," and "Purpose." I am hoping one day these songs of triumph, adoration, and praise to God will be recorded. I can totally relate to Mary's song of triumph, which is also referred to as "The Magnificat." It is a beautiful hymn from Mary dedicated to God. In her song of triumph, Mary expresses praise, adoration, exultation, and gratitude to God for the marvelous, miraculous work that He chose to perform in and through her life. While meditating on Mary's song of triumph, or "The Magnificat," there are three key things that stand out about it.

First: Mary starts her song worshipping God for who He is! There is a difference between worship and praise. Worship is when we actively reverence God for who He is. Praise is when we boast about or celebrate what God has done. In Mary's song, she not only worships God for who He is, but she makes it personal by declaring who He is to her. Let's examine the opening of Mary's song. She says, "My soul magnifies the Lord, and my spirit has rejoiced in God my Savior." Mankind is a triune being—consisting of spirit, soul, and body. The soul is a person's mind, will, and emotions. Therefore, Mary tells God with her innermost being, (her mind, her will, and her emotions). She makes Him great above all things! She highly esteems, extols, and celebrates who He is! She does this because first of all, He is Lord. Mary acknowledges this and also gives God this rightful position in her life.

According to *The Strong's Exhaustive Concordance of the Bible*, "Lord" is the Greek word *kyrios*, which means Master, controller, and supreme in authority. Mary not only acknowledges God as

God but also as her personal Savior. Worship is personal! Worship is intimacy with God! Worship is humbling oneself before God. Worship brings us into the very presence of God! James 4:8 (KJV) tells us, *"Draw nigh to God, and He will draw nigh to you…"* How do we draw nigh to God? James tells us, with a contrite heart, a heart that is humble and repentant because it acknowledges God's holiness. Like Mary, we, too must understand the importance of worshipping God, especially when He manifests His will, plan, and presence in our lives.

Second: Mary gives her testimony of what God has done for her. Mary says, *"For He has regarded the lowly state of His maidservant; for behold, henceforth all generations will call me blessed. For He who is mighty has done great things for me….."* Luke 1:48-49 (NKJV). Mary recognizes it was not because she was affluent, wealthy, well-known, or the best-qualified according to man's standards that God chose her. Instead, God "regarded" her lowly state. According to *The Strong's Exhaustive Concordance of the Bible*, the word "regarded" here is the Greek word *epiblepō,* which means to turn the eyes upon, to look upon, and to gaze at (with favor). In the eyes of man, Mary's meager state would not be something to notice or even gaze at with favor. Rather, her lowly state would be something to look down on. Mary's meager state was also probably quite humiliating. But God saw that lowly state as the perfect position and condition to work out His master plan. Aren't you glad God's standards are not the same as man's standards?

When God reveals and then fulfills His will and purpose for your life, like Mary, you, too will have a personal song of triumph! You, too will have a personal testimony of how God has done great things for you. Your personal song will be about how when everyone else counted you out and thought you would never amount to anything, God "regarded" you! God looked upon you with favor. Your song will be about how God took what other people regarded as trash (such as your status in life, your state in life) and turned it into treasure! Just one touch of God's favor will take you from the bottom all the way to the top! Just one touch of God's favor will take you from the backroom to the boardroom! Just one touch of God's favor will make your name a household name throughout all generations like Mary, the Mother of Jesus!

Lastly: Mary prophesies about what God was about to do for her people, the nation of Israel, as a result of her conception of the long-awaited Messiah! For four hundred years, God had been silent. For four hundred years, the nation of Israel had been taken into captivity by one nation after another. These nations oppressed the Israelites. However, God, who is holy, God, who cannot lie, God, who is merciful, and who is faithful to His promises, had finally sent the Savior of His people. The Savior, in the person of Jesus Christ, was going to exalt His oppressed people. He was going to scatter the proud and put down the oppressors of His people. These were the very things that God promised He would do for Abraham and his descendants. Mary knew that with the birth of the Messiah, everything that God had declared through His prophets concerning His people was already done!

I truly believe Mary's song, King David's songs, Hannah's song, and my songs were put in our minds and hearts by God to minister unto Him. Let's think about it. We were created for God's pleasure. Revelation 4:11 (KJV) declares *"Thou art worthy, O Lord, to receive glory and honour and power: for thou hast created all things, and for thy pleasure they are and were created."* God knows what pleases Him, and I know He gives us songs to sing to Him. According to the Bible, God is a singer. Zephaniah 3:17 (KJV) says that *"...he will joy over thee with singing."* What a wonderful image of God singing over you and me!

The Bible tells us in Jeremiah 29:11 (NIV), *"For I know the plans I have for you," declares the Lord, "plans to prosper you and not to harm you, plans to give you hope and a future."* My brothers and sisters in Christ, it truly does not matter how humble your beginnings or where you are in life, God knows where to find you! At the appointed time when He reveals His awesome plans for your life, you need to agree with Him. You need to agree with everything God says about you and agree with what He says He has equipped you to do. Take courage and submit to His will! His plans are going to be far beyond your resources, your abilities, and your qualifications. This is how you will know it's God's plan! When you do all these things, you will come forth triumphantly. Then, you, too will have a song of triumph like Mary, a poor girl who became the Mother of Life!

About ZION Publishing House

ZION Publishing House is a family-owned publishing company based in Washington, DC and South Dakota. ZION helps Christian authors tell their stories by providing an affordable alternative to traditional publishing. Our mission is to maintain a platform that educates and empowers independent Christian authors. We do this by cultivating talent in the inspirational and self-help genres for novice and experienced authors. The path to publishing can be daunting and extremely complex. We take pride in taking our clients by the hand and walking them through the publishing process to ensure they not only have a high-quality product that resonates with the reader, but they understand the many facets of the publishing industry and what it means to be a published author.

If you are a writer looking for an affordable path to high-quality publishing, visit our website at **www.zionpublishinghouse.com** to learn more.

www.ingramcontent.com/pod-product-compliance
Lightning Source LLC
Chambersburg PA
CBHW021638080526
44584CB00015BA/1529